THE BASIS
CHRISTIAN
UNITY

THE BASIS OF CHRISTIAN UNITY

D. M. Lloyd-Jones

THE BANNER OF TRUTH TRUST

THE BANNER OF TRUTH TRUST
3 Murrayfield Road, Edinburgh EH12 6EL
P.O. Box 621, Carlisle, Pennsylvania 17013, USA

*

© Lady Catherwood and Mrs Ann Beatt 2003

Previously published in *Knowing the Times: Addresses
Delivered on Various Occasions 1942–77,* 1989
This edition first published 2003

*

ISBN 0 85151 846 X

*

Typeset in 12/16 pt New Baskerville at
the Banner of Truth Trust, Edinburgh
Printed and bound in Great Britain by
Creative Print & Design (Wales)
Ebbw Vale

Contents

Publisher's Preface

In June 1962, Dr Martyn Lloyd-Jones addressed the Westminster Fellowship on Christian unity, a topic then receiving a great deal of attention as the ecumenical movement gained momentum. The substance of his two addresses was published by Inter-Varsity Press in December that year.

Dr Lloyd-Jones' approach was to show from John 17 and Ephesians 4, the two passages most frequently appealed to in this connection, that Christian unity was the result of a shared faith in the gospel of Christ, not something arrived at by ignoring or minimizing truth.[1]

The ecumenical debate has moved on, but the basic issues remain the same, and Dr Lloyd-Jones' lucid examination of them here is of abiding value.

August 2003

[1] For the background see Iain H. Murray, *D. M. Lloyd-Jones: The Fight of Faith, 1939–81* (Edinburgh: Banner of Truth, 1990), especially Chapter 21, *Unity: Ecumenical or Evangelical?*

1

Introduction

No question is receiving so much attention at the present time in all branches and divisions of the Christian church as the question of church unity.[1] It is being written about, talked about, and preached about. Now we are all agreed, surely, that the Christian church should be one, that she was meant by God to be one. And therefore we must agree, further, that it is a tragedy that division ever entered into the life of the church. In addition, we must all regard schism as a grievous sin. That is common ground. But having said that, one must also point out that there is obviously great confusion, and much disagreement, as to what constitutes unity, as to what the nature of unity is, and as to how unity is to be obtained and preserved.

[1] What follows is the substance of two addresses to the Westminster Fellowship in June 1962 previously published in D. M. Lloyd-Jones, *Knowing the Times: Addresses Delivered on Various Occasions 1942–77* (Edinburgh: Banner of Truth, 1989), pp. 118–63).

1. Some Current Views

There are many divergent views with regard to this. The Roman Catholic solution to the problem, of necessity, and in spite of what appears to be greater friendliness at the present time, is simply absorption into her institution and organization. *Semper eadem* is her great slogan: the church is 'always the same'. From her standpoint, and on the basis of her definition, it must be. Therefore it is quite logical that her notion of unity should be that all other sections of the church should return to her who is 'the one and only true church of Christ'. The so-called 'Orthodox' churches, Greek and Russian, hold a similar view.

But there are other views, some of which contrast sharply with this in their looseness. The commonest of these maintains that what is desired is a visible unity and coming together of all who call themselves Christian in any sense whatsoever. Unity means that all sections of the Christian church, anybody, everybody claiming the name of Christian, should meet together, have fellowship together, and work together, presenting a common front to the enemies of Christianity.

One other view must be especially mentioned at this point as it seems to be becoming fairly popular in evangelical circles. This regards unity in terms of coming together to form a kind of 'forum', where various views of the Christian faith may be 'discussed' and people may present their different 'insights', in the hope that as a

result they may eventually arrive at some common
agreement. There are other views, but let that suffice as a
broad classification.

2. The Limits of This Study

This subject is exceedingly complex and many volumes
have been written about it. My objective in this paper is a
very limited one; it is to examine the two passages of
Scripture which are most frequently quoted in this connection. I refer, of course, to John 17 and Ephesians 4,
and in particular to John 17:21 and Ephesians 4:13. These
are the verses that are so frequently quoted today and
used as slogans, statements which apparently settle the
matter once and for all and place it beyond any dispute
or discussion. It is essential, therefore, that we should
examine them very carefully.

I propose to examine them in the light of certain questions. First: What is the nature or the character of true
unity? Secondly: What is the place of doctrine and belief
in this matter of unity? Thirdly: How does unity come
into being?

Attention is focused mainly on the third question
because of its practical character. The majority view holds
that the way to produce unity is not to discuss and consider doctrine, but rather to work together and to pray
together. The slogans are that 'doctrine divides', but that
as we 'work together' and 'pray together' we shall arrive
at unity. This becomes serious when it is applied to the
question of evangelism. The commonest argument used

to press upon us the vital and urgent importance of this question of unity is that evangelism is impossible apart from it, that the divided church is an offence to the world, and that while we are divided the world will not listen to us. Therefore, we are told, it is urgently essential that we should come together in order that we may evangelize. We have been told frequently that at this point of evangelism we can surely all be one.

During an evangelistic campaign in London a few years ago a weekly paper, now defunct, calling itself *The Christian World*, carried the heading, 'Let us have a theological truce during the Campaign'. A well-known evangelistic leader has also committed himself to this: 'We can all at any rate be ecumenical in evangelism.' That it is only after the stage of evangelism that you begin to consider doctrine is a very common and prevailing view.

All this obviously makes it of vital importance that we should be clear in our thinking on these questions which I have raised with regard to the basis of Christian unity. It is essential, therefore, that these key passages should be carefully studied. It is also my aim to show that the general tenor of New Testament teaching supports and confirms the proper interpretation of these two passages. This will be dealt with in Chapter 4.

2

The Teaching
of John 17

John 17:21 is the verse which is so frequently used as a slogan. In it our Lord prays, 'That they all may be one; as thou, Father, art in me, and I in thee, that they also may be one in us: that the world may believe that thou hast sent me.'

How do we interpret it? We do so, first of all, by taking it in its context and setting. This is a principle which should always govern scriptural exposition. The charge that has been so frequently hurled against evangelicals is that they are fond of using 'proof-texts'. That is the criticism brought against the Westminster Confession and, indeed, most of the confessions. They are based, it is said, on proof-texts. We are told that we must never do that, that we must take the general tenor and sense of

Scripture and not base our position upon particular texts; but advocates of the ecumenical movement have done precisely that with regard to this verse. They have taken it entirely out of its context and then proceeded to use it as a slogan. Over against this we assert that it is always wrong to take a text in isolation. The first rule of interpretation is that a text should always be considered in its context, and, in addition, compared with other texts. If ever that canon of interpretation was important it is in connection with this particular statement.

1. The Context Analysed

We start, therefore, by giving a general analysis of the seventeenth chapter of John's Gospel. It falls into several obvious sections. The first section consists of the first five verses, where our Lord is praying chiefly for Himself. The second section consists of verses 6 to 10 in which He gives a description of His people, for whom He is praying, and offers a general prayer for them.

Then in verses 11 and 12 He offers the fundamental prayer that they may be kept as one. In verses 13 to 16 He prays in particular that they may be kept as one against the subtle attacks of the evil one who is always anxious to disrupt this essential unity.

In verses 17 to 19 He prays for their sanctification, again in order that they may be kept in the truth and in this unity. In verses 20 to 23 He takes up what He has already prayed in verse 11 and elaborates it in order to define in more detail the nature of the unity.

And in verses 24 to 26 He gives expression to His ultimate desire for His people, that they may be where He is,
that they may behold the glory which the Father has given
Him. That is the general analysis of the whole section.

2. Principles of Unity

As we come to a more detailed consideration of this question of unity we notice that the first specific mention of it
is in verse 11. Our Lord says, 'And now I am no more in
the world, but these are in the world, and I come to thee.
Holy Father, keep through thine own name those whom
thou hast given me, that they may be one, as we are.' That
is the fundamental text, and in that one statement we
have all the essential principles stated.

i. Its Restricted Reference

First, we notice that He is praying for particular people
whom He designates as 'these'. They, and they alone, are
the subject of this unity. Who are 'these'? In the chapter
itself there are many answers to this question. 'These' are
the people of whom He has said right at the beginning
that they have been given to Him by God. That is a fundamental statement, which He goes on repeating. There
are certain people who belong to God, whom God the
Father has given to Him, and for whose sake He has come
into the world and has done what He has done.

Another thing He says about them is that they are
people who have been separated from the world. 'I pray

for them: I pray not for the world, but for them which thou hast given me; for they are thine', He says in verse 9. That is a very important statement. Here are people who have been taken out of the world, separated from it; and it is for these, and for these alone, that He prays. There is no 'universalism' in this chapter. There is nothing here to suggest that the work that our Lord did in this world was done for everybody, and that, though there may be some who do not realize it and do not know it while they are in this world, it is nevertheless true of them, and ultimately all are to be saved. On the contrary, there is a clear-cut division and distinction between those who are still in the world and those whom He has called out of the world.

We have a still more interesting and important definition as to who 'these' are in verses 6–8: 'I have manifested thy name unto the men which thou gavest me out of the world: thine they were, and thou gavest them me; and they have kept thy word. Now they have known that all things whatsoever thou hast given me are of thee. For I have given unto them the words which thou gavest me; and they have received them, and have known surely that I came out from thee, and they have believed that thou didst send me.'

This is of crucial importance. So much so that our Lord brings out the same idea again in verse 20, where we have: 'Neither pray I for these alone, but for them also which shall believe on me through their word.' These have believed on Him and His Word; others are going to believe on Him through the same Word which these are now going to speak in the world. The emphasis is the same. He repeats it again in verse 25; this is the final definition of these people: 'O righteous Father, the world hath not known thee: but I have known thee, and these have known that thou hast sent me.' This is a most important statement because it further defines who these people are.

What, then, are the characteristics of these people? Again we must emphasize the element of separation and distinction. Our Lord does not pray for the world; He prays only for these people who have been given to Him. Indeed He says specifically in verse 19: 'And for their sakes I sanctify myself, that they also might be sanctified through the truth.' That is a reference, of course, to His giving Himself, setting Himself apart for His death, for the work of atonement and reconciliation; and there He specifically says that He does not do that for everybody, He does it for 'these' people only. Again, a most important statement.

In other words these people who are the subjects of the unity of which our Lord is speaking are not those who happen to have been brought up in a certain country, or who happen to belong to a given race or nation or a particular visible church. They are those who have 'received' His Word, His teaching, and particularly His teaching concerning Himself. They have known who He is, that He has been sent by God, and that He has been sent to do this work for them. They have 'believed' and have 'received' that Word. That is His own definition of these people. In other words, the unity of which He is speaking applies only to those who receive and believe this Word, what we now would call the gospel message.

ii. Its Origin

The second principle which He lays down in the eleventh verse concerns the origin of the unity. You notice that He uses the word 'keep'. 'Holy Father,' He says, 'keep through thine own name those whom thou hast given me.' Nowhere in this chapter is there an exhortation or an appeal to produce a unity. Our Lord is saying that the unity is already there, already in existence. It is the unity of those who, in contradistinction to all others, have believed the truth concerning Him and His work.

Our Lord, knowing that He is now about to leave the world and that they are going to be exposed to the attack of the evil one and all the forces of temptation of sin and evil, is praying to His Father to keep them in the unity that already exists. That, I repeat, is a very important point and principle. Our Lord is not dealing with something at which we should aim. Indeed our Lord does not address His disciples at all in this chapter. It is a prayer to God to keep the unity that He, through His preaching, has already brought into existence among these people.

iii. Its Nature

The third point which our Lord raises is that of the nature of the unity: 'That they may be one, as we are.' This is the fundamental text, as it were, on the subject, but as our Lord elaborates it in verses 20 to 23, let us now proceed to consider them: 'Neither pray I for these alone, but for them also which shall believe on me through their word; that they all may be one; as thou, Father, art in me, and I in thee, that they also may be one in us: that the world may believe that thou hast sent me. And the glory which thou gavest me I have given them; that they may be one, even as we are one: I in them, and thou in me, that they may be made perfect in one; and that the world may know that thou hast sent me, and hast loved them, as thou hast loved me.'

Here we have what is undoubtedly one of the most exalted statements to be found anywhere in the whole of the Scriptures. We notice at once that the essential character of the unity about which our Lord is speaking is that it is comparable to the unity that exists between the Father and the Son. It is also comparable to the unity between the Son and the people for whom He is praying.

Light is thrown on this in certain verses of John 14. For instance, in verse 20 our Lord says: 'At that day ye shall know that I am in my Father, and ye in me, and I in you'; and in verse 21: 'He that hath my commandments, and keepeth them, he it is that loveth me: and he that loveth me shall be loved of my Father, and I will love him, and will manifest myself to him.' Verse 23 continues: 'If a man love me, he will keep my words: and my Father will love him, and we will come unto him, and make our abode with him.'

Now whatever else may be said of the verses we are examining in chapter 17, it is quite obvious that this statement is not one to be handled lightly, glibly, or loosely, as if its meaning were perfectly clear and self-evident. Our Lord is dealing here with the mystical union which subsists between the three persons of the blessed Holy Trinity. It is the highest mystery of the Christian faith. And yet this is the term, the verse, that is being bandied about as if its meaning were obvious, and indeed as if it had but one meaning, namely, some external organizational unity.

Everything about the statement indicates the exact opposite. It is concerned with a unity of essence. That is the whole mystery of the Trinity. There are three persons and yet but one God. The same essence and yet the distinctions in the persons. But what makes them one is the unity of essence. That cannot be excluded. Of course, in addition to that, there is the unity of outlook and of thought and of purpose, the mutual love, and everything else that follows of necessity from it. Now that is the way in which our Lord Himself defines this unity which already obtains among His people and which He prays God to preserve and to keep after His return to glory.

We deduce from this that the unity which is to obtain in the church is something which involves this unity of essence, of being. This is, of course, only another way of putting the doctrine taught so plainly in the New Testament that the Christian is a man who is 'born again', 'born of the Spirit', a 'partaker of the divine nature'. All that is implicit here. We must be careful because the subject is difficult. We must never teach that the Christian is made divine, but the scriptural phrase as used by Peter is that we are made 'partakers of the divine nature' (*2 Pet.* 1:4). There is no unity at all in our Lord's sense apart from this fundamental operation of the Holy Spirit of God, who creates within the believers of the truth this new nature. And that in turn leads, by the same analogy, to an identity of view, of object, of love, and so on.

In other words, the unity that our Lord is talking about is a unity that clearly can obtain only among those who are regenerate or born again. It is not something, by definition, that one can decide to go in for. It is not like a number of people deciding to form a coalition or a society in order that certain objects and purposes should be carried out. I am not saying that there is anything wrong in that. My concern is to show that that is not what our Lord was talking about. It is not even a matter of friendship. It is deeper than that. It is like a family relationship. You have no choice about it and what it involves. You are born into a family. Though you may disagree with members of your family you cannot get rid of the relationship. It is a matter of blood and of essence. So is the unity of the church. It must never be thought of, therefore, as something voluntary. It is something which is inevitable because it is the result of being born into a given family. Christians are brothers and not merely an association of friends.

3. Summary

To sum up the teaching of this passage before we turn to the other: our Lord is praying here that this unity which

He has brought into being, and which He has Himself preserved while He was still with the disciples, may be continued. Incidentally, it is interesting to notice that He mentions that extraordinary exception, the case of Judas. Here is one who belonged to the company but who shows quite clearly that he is not truly 'of' it. Verse 12 says: 'While I was with them in the world, I kept them in thy name: those that thou gavest me I have kept, and none of them is lost, but the son of perdition; that the scripture might be fulfilled.' You may give the appearance of belonging, but if there is not this new life and this new birth there is no real unity; and it must eventually show itself.

So we find here that the whole of our Lord's statement is not an exhortation to us to do anything, but is a prayer to His Father asking Him to preserve this unity that is already in existence. Moreover that unity is essentially spiritual, is produced by the operation of the Holy Spirit in the act of regeneration, and shows itself in a common belief and reception of the teaching concerning our Lord's Person and work. Any 'unity' which lacks these characteristics is not the unity of which our Lord speaks in John 17.

3

The Teaching
of Ephesians 4

The second crucial passage with which we are concerned is Ephesians 4:1–16. In many respects it runs parallel to the one we have already looked at, the one big difference being that it is an exhortation addressed to Christian believers rather than a prayer which is offered to God. For this reason we shall devote the major part of our space to its consideration.

1. Does Fellowship or Doctrine Come First?

What does this passage teach? There are many who think that the teaching here is that we are exhorted to have fellowship with one another, whatever our views of the Christian faith may be, in order that ultimately we may come to a unity of faith and belief.

Some years ago a well-known evangelical preacher put it like this: 'I always used to think that you could not have fellowship with a man unless you were agreed with him about doctrine. My position had always been that first of all you must have agreement about truth and your view of truth, and then, on that basis, you could have fellowship with people.' But he went on to say that he had made a great and startling discovery from reading again this fourth chapter of the Epistle to the Ephesians. He had observed for the first time in his life that the apostle starts by exhorting to fellowship: 'Endeavouring to keep the unity of the Spirit in the bond of peace' (verse 3). He said, 'I discovered that there you start with fellowship and it is only later, in verse 13, that the apostle says, "Till we all come in the unity of the faith, and of the knowledge of the Son of God, unto a perfect man, unto the measure of the stature of the fulness of Christ."'

So in the light of that he was now proposing to have fellowship with people who disagreed with him theologically, those who were liberal in their doctrinal outlook, and others. He was going to do this because he believed it was through such fellowship that he could hope to arrive ultimately at doctrinal agreement. It was a complete reversal of the position that he had before held. He felt convicted, he felt he had been sinful. And now he exhorts Christian people to put his new view of the teaching of Ephesians 4 into practice. It is through working together, evangelizing together, praying together, and having fellowship together, he declares, that we shall ultimately arrive at the unity of the faith.

The crucial question we must consider is whether this section of Scripture teaches that or not. Again the context is absolutely vital, and we must therefore begin by making a general analysis of the passage. The theme, quite clearly, is the unity of the church. Indeed that has been the theme of the apostle right from the beginning of the Epistle. In many ways the key verse to an understanding of the whole letter is 1:10: 'That in the dispensation of the fulness of times he might gather together in one all things in Christ, both which are in heaven, and which are on earth; even in him.' The apostle proceeds to show how God has been doing this by bringing the Jew and the Gentile together in this one new body, which is the church, and then calls attention in particular to this theme in the section we are examining.

A general analysis of the section reveals the following: in verses 1 to 3 Paul makes a general appeal for unity; in verses 4 to 6 he describes the nature of the unity; in verses 7 to 12 he describes the variety in the unity and the means which God has taken to preserve it; finally, in verses 13 to 16, he describes the unity perfected, or its ultimate full realization and flowering. This he presents both positively and negatively.

The key to the whole exposition of Ephesians chapter 4 is the word 'therefore' in verse 1. It points us back to the first three chapters of this great Epistle, and emphasizes that the theme of unity is something which follows as a consequence of what has gone before. This, of course, is typical of the New Testament method of dealing with matters of conduct and practice. Its essential teaching is that conduct is always the outcome of truth and of teaching. Practice and behaviour are the result of the application of doctrine which has already been laid down. And that is precisely what the apostle does here. 'Therefore', he says, 'I therefore, the prisoner of the Lord, beseech you that ye walk worthy of the vocation wherewith ye are called.' The exhortation that follows is made in the light of all that he has been saying in the first three chapters.

It is clear, then, that anyone who interprets this section as saying that the apostle starts with fellowship and then goes on to doctrine is fundamentally wrong. Such a person's entire exposition is vitiated at the outset, for the simple reason that he starts with verse 3 and ignores verses 1 and 2. The doctrine expounded in chapters 1 to 3 is already the basis and the background of everything the apostle has to say about unity. He does not start with unity and then proceed to doctrine; he takes up unity because he has already laid down his doctrine.

2. The Context of Ephesians 4

The apostle makes this abundantly clear in his opening exhortation that we are to 'walk worthy of the vocation wherewith [we] are called'. Now the word 'worthy' brings together two main ideas. One is 'equal weight', 'balance'. In other words he is saying, You have already heard what the doctrine is; now you must balance that with your practice and conduct. You have exactly the same thought in Hebrews 6:11: 'And we desire', says the writer there, 'that . . . you do shew the same diligence.' They had been showing diligence in their practical works of helping one another, so he says, in effect, We exhort you now to show the same diligence in the matter of the full assurance of hope to the end. In other words it is again a matter of balance, balance between doctrine and practice.

The second notion in this word is the idea of something that 'becomes' or 'fits in with' something else. Philippians 1:27 conveys exactly the idea: 'Only let your conversation be as it becometh the gospel of Christ.' You have your doctrine, Paul says; now be careful that your conversation becomes it, that it corresponds to it, that it does not clash with it, that it fits in with it, that it shows it out still more in its glory and in its perfection.

Another well-known phrase in the letter to Titus puts it like this: 'Adorn the doctrine' (*Titus* 2:10). That is what conduct and practice are meant to do. We must not think of them apart from doctrine. To talk about unity apart from doctrine is like talking about a woman's clothing as if it had no connection with her person. The business of the clothing is to adorn the person. So it is with practice and doctrine. One is to adorn the other. This is quite fundamental in all approaches to this question of unity.

Then to make it still more specific the apostle says that we are to walk worthy of the vocation, or calling, wherewith we are called. What does he mean by this repetition of the word 'call'? He is referring here to the whole plan of salvation as he has already outlined it in the earlier chapters. It is not simply a matter of 'living up to your calling' as the New English Bible puts it. It involves the whole doctrine of the 'call', and to understand what is in the apostle's mind we must go back to the earlier part of the Epistle.

3. A Summary of Ephesians 1–3

Briefly we can put it like this. In verses 9 and 10 of chapter 1 the apostle outlines the plan and the purpose of salvation in the general statement: 'Having made known unto us the mystery of his will, according to his good pleasure which he hath purposed in himself: that in the dispensation of the fulness of times he might gather together in one all things in Christ, both which are in heaven, and which are on earth; even in him.' That is the great eternal purpose of God which, as Paul has already told us in verse 4, has been planned 'before the foundation of the world': 'According as he hath chosen us in him before the foundation of the world.'

This purpose has been carried out through everything that has happened in and through our Lord and Saviour Jesus Christ. (Notice the repetition of the words 'Jesus Christ', 'Christ', 'in him', throughout this entire section in the first chapter.) In particular, salvation is through the blood of Christ, 'in whom we have redemption through his blood, the forgiveness of sins, according to the riches of his grace' (verse 7). That is the great doctrine stated in general. There is no unity, there can be no unity, apart from the person of the Lord Jesus Christ, apart from His work and especially apart from the redemption which is 'through his blood'. That is essential to the only unity in which the New Testament is interested, and which it defines so clearly.

The question now arises, How does anyone ever come into this unity? The apostle tells us in 1:4–6: 'According as he hath chosen us in him before the foundation of the world, that we should be holy and without blame before him in love: having predestinated us unto the adoption of children by Jesus Christ to himself, according to the good pleasure of his will, to the praise of the glory of his grace, wherein he hath made us accepted in the beloved.' That is the great source of all unity. That is how men enter into it, and it must never be thought of apart from this great, high, and exalted doctrine. Paul expresses the same thought in verse 11: 'In whom also we have obtained an inheritance, being predestinated according to the purpose of him who worketh all things after the counsel of his own will.'

In practice and experience we enter into this unity through the process described in 1:12–13. In verse 12 he talks about the Jews: 'That we should be to the praise of his glory, who first trusted in Christ.' That is how the Jews came in; they had placed their trust in Christ. Then in verse 13 he turns to the Gentile Ephesians: 'In whom ye also trusted, after that ye heard the word of truth, the gospel of your salvation', and, 'In whom also after that ye believed . . .'. In practice we come into it as the result of hearing this word of the gospel of the Lord Jesus Christ and believing it, trusting it, putting our faith utterly and entirely in it and in Him. That is the essential message of the first chapter.

In the second chapter the apostle elaborates all this, putting it still more plainly. Who are these people whom he is exhorting to continue in unity? They are those who have realized that by nature they were dead in trespasses and sins. That is the vital statement in chapter 2, verse 1. They realize further that they are under the dominion and the control of the devil, 'the prince of the power of the air', and rebels against God (verse 2). They realize also that they are the slaves of their own lusts and passions. And still more important and significant, they realize that they are under the wrath of God, that they, like everybody else, are 'the children of wrath' (verse 3).

In other words, these people believe in the fact and the doctrine of the Fall of man. They realize that they are spiritually dead, under the condemnation of God and His holy law, and that they can do nothing about their salvation and reconciliation to God. They realize, furthermore, that they are now Christians, members of God's church, solely because of what God has done to them through the Holy Spirit: 'you hath he quickened'. They realize that God has quickened them by the Spirit, put new life into them, given them the ability to see the truth as it is in Christ Jesus, and to believe it.

Furthermore, Paul tells us that they are people who are united to Christ. They have been quickened together with Christ', they have been 'raised together' with Him, and they have been 'made to sit together in heavenly places in Christ Jesus' (verses 4–7). And in order to make the thing clear beyond any doubt he goes on to say, 'For by grace are ye saved through faith; and that not of yourselves: it is the gift of God: not of works, lest any man should boast. For we are his workmanship, created in Christ Jesus unto good works, which God hath before ordained that we should walk in them' (verses 8–10).

In other words the people whom the apostle is exhorting to 'keep' this unity of faith are those who have been 'regenerated', who are God's 'workmanship'. They are what they are as the result of what God has done to them and in them.

But he does not leave it even at that. In 2:13–16 he reminds these Ephesian Christians that they are people who have realized that all their own good works, all their good living, all their activities, their nationality, their religion, and everything they had before, are entirely useless, and that they are made Christian, and brought into this unity which is in the church, entirely by the action of the Lord Jesus Christ, and particularly by the shedding of His blood upon the cross: 'But now in Christ Jesus ye who sometimes were far off are made nigh by the blood of Christ. For he is our peace, who hath made both one, and hath broken down the middle wall of partition between us; having abolished in his flesh the enmity, even the law of commandments contained in ordinances; for to make in himself of twain one new man, so making peace; and that he might reconcile both unto

God in one body by the cross, having slain the enmity thereby.'

These, and these alone, are the subjects of the unity of which he speaks in chapter 4. That is how these people have been brought into the unity. It is entirely wrong to start with unity as a separate concept. It is something that results from all that has gone before. As we have already pointed out, the word 'therefore' in 4:1 points back to all these matters which are elaborated in such detail in the second chapter. These people are those who have been 'bought' into God's kingdom and family at the cost of 'the precious blood of Christ'. No-one can ever belong to this family, and participate in its unity, unless he believes that.

The apostle then goes on to say that it is only because of this that we can pray. 'For through him we both have access by one Spirit unto the Father' (2:18). There is only one way in which any man can pray and that is 'through' the Lord Jesus Christ 'by' the Holy Spirit. A man cannot have access to the Father except 'by the blood of Christ'. Hebrews 10:19 teaches us the same thing. It is the teaching of the whole of the New Testament: 'God heareth not sinners' (*John* 9:31). It is only by relying upon the blood of Christ, by believing that His blood was shed for us and for our sins, that God 'made him to be sin for us, who knew no sin' (*2 Cor.* 5:21), and punished our sins in Him, that we have access to the Father. And it is the Holy Spirit who enables us, in the light of it, to have this access to the Father. The apostle ends this chapter by saying that the people whom he is exhorting to continue in this unity are those who, as the result of all this, are now fellow citizens, and members together of the household of God, and are established together and 'built [together] upon the foundation of the apostles and prophets', which means the teaching and the doctrine of the apostles and prophets. And because they are on this foundation they have become 'a habitation of God' who dwells in them. That is a summary of the teaching of the second chapter.

The third chapter tells us how this great plan and purpose of God had been revealed to the apostle and includes his prayer that these Ephesian believers should enter more fully into an understanding of all this. It is a glorious chapter. It is not essential to our present purpose that we should go into it in detail. His prayer for the Ephesians is that they, together with all other saints, may be led by the Spirit into an even fuller understanding of what God has made possible for them in and through the Lord Jesus Christ.

So he starts this fourth chapter which we are considering. That is the calling wherewith they are called, nothing less than that. It is not simply that a man thinks he is a Christian or decides to be a Christian. He is a man who has been called effectually by the Spirit of God into this position and relationship through believing the truth which has been presented to him. The apostle is concerned, as he has said in 1:18, that the Holy Spirit may 'enlighten the eyes of the understanding' of these people in order that they may enter into a fuller and deeper comprehension of this wonderful truth.

4. The Unity of All Who Are 'in Christ'

That, then, is the character of the people who are the subjects of the unity which the apostle now proceeds to consider. He is writing to such, and to nobody else. What is his appeal to them? We have it in verses 2 and 3: 'With all lowliness and meekness, with longsuffering, forbearing one another in love; endeavouring to keep the unity of the Spirit in the bond of peace.' He says that we should show 'great diligence eagerly'. To what end? Not to produce a unity, not to create a unity, not to try to arrive at a unity, but to 'keep the unity'. Again, it is the same fundamental point which we noticed in our exposition of the passage in John 17. The unity is already in existence. It is the unity of all those who have believed the message expounded in chapters 1 to 3. As our Lord had prophesied in His prayer recorded in John 17, there were to be people who would believe the message of the apostles whom He was sending out. And here is one of the apostles writing to Ephesians who have believed, who have 'received' that message. And because of that they are in this body, they are one with all others who believe the same message; and the exhortation is that they should 'keep', should preserve, this unity.

That is the way in which the New Testament always puts it. The unity itself is inevitable among all those who have been quickened by the Holy Spirit out of spiritual death and given new life in Christ Jesus. What they have to be careful about is that they do not allow anything to disrupt it or in any way to interfere with it. The emphasis is entirely upon the word 'keep'.

In order that this may be abundantly clear the apostle again reminds us that it is 'the unity of the Spirit'. In other words, it is a unity which is produced by the Holy Spirit and by Him alone. Man cannot produce this, try as he may. Because of the nature of this unity, because it is a spiritual unity, it can be brought into being only as a result of the operation of the Holy Spirit. The apostle rejoices in this staggering fact, that these people who were once Jews and Gentiles are now one in Christ Jesus. They not only share the same life, they are agreed about their doctrine. They believe the same things, they are trusting to the same person, and they know that He has saved them all in the same way. The middle wall of partition has gone. The Jews no longer pride themselves that they are Jews and that they had the law given to them, whereas the Gentiles were ignorant and were not in the unique position of being the people of God. All these differences have gone, and they are one in seeing their lost estate and condition, their utter hopelessness and helplessness. They are united in their common trust in the Lord Jesus Christ, the Son of God, who has purchased them at the cost of His own precious blood. So they are ready to listen to this exhortation which urges them to maintain with great diligence, to preserve and to guard, the unity into which they have been brought by the operation of the Holy Spirit of God.

5. The Nature of Spiritual Unity

That leads us to our next question: What, then, is the nature of the unity produced by the Spirit? The answer is supplied in verses 4 to 6: 'There is one body, and one Spirit, even as ye are called in one hope of your calling; one Lord, one faith, one baptism, one God and Father of all, who is above all, and through all, and in you all.' Notice again the exalted way in which the unity is described. This is not just a question of friendliness or fellowship, of good nature, or of desiring to do good together. It is something, once more, which lifts us up into the realm of the blessed Holy Trinity, the Spirit, the Son, the Father! The unity must always be conceived of in this exalted way and never merely in terms of human fellowship, or co-operation, or organization.

Observe that the word 'one' is used seven times in these three verses. At the beginning of verse 4 the Authorized Version translators have supplied the words 'There is'. The words in the original are, 'Endeavouring to keep the unity of the Spirit in the bond of peace. One body . . .'. The apostle puts it baldly because the thing is beyond dispute. The translators rightly supplied the words, 'There is', which help to emphasize that fact. 'There is but one body', and it is this body that has been produced by the Holy Spirit. Unity is already there, he says. We must get rid entirely of the notion that the Ephesians are being exhorted to produce or to arrive at something. '*There is*', he says; you are already enjoying it; all you have to do is to preserve it!

The first thing we are told about the nature of this unity is that it is the kind of unity that is found in a physical body. That is clearly the apostle's favourite analogy in this connection. He has already used it in 1:22 and 23. He has reminded us of it again in 2:16. We shall find it again in 4:16. He works it out *in extenso* in Romans 12 and in 1 Corinthians 12.

Why is this such a good analogy? For the obvious reason that it emphasizes the vital and organic character of the unity. It is not just a loose grouping, or a mechanical or external attachment. The whole marvel and mystery of the human body is that, while it consists of so many different parts, all with their various functions, they are all one; they are bound together in a vital manner.

It is not a question of fingers being stuck on to hands, and hands to forearms, and so on. It is all one. All the parts come out of an original cell, as it were, an original germ of life, and they are all extensions and manifestations of this. The unity in the church is like that and, whether we like it or not, we have to face this fact.

Paul goes on to compare this with the unity that characterizes the life of the blessed Holy Trinity, the mystical union between the Father, the Son, and the Holy Spirit. 'There is one body,' he says, 'and one Spirit . . . one Lord . . . one God and Father of all.' Three in one, one in three. That is the kind of unity about which the apostle is speaking, and he now proceeds to indicate in greater detail the character of the unity in terms of the part played by the three Persons in its production.

1. 'ONE SPIRIT, EVEN AS YE ARE CALLED IN ONE HOPE OF YOUR CALLING'

It is the peculiar work of the Spirit to 'call' us into this unity. He does so, of course, by convicting us, by quickening us, by enabling us to believe. He enters into us. He baptizes us into the body of Christ (*1 Cor.* 12:13). He then enlightens our understanding and leads us on. We enjoy His fellowship.

The apostle is particularly concerned to emphasize the 'calling' of Christians, the results of this call worked by the Holy Spirit, and the effectual character of this work. He does so in many places. For example in 1 Corinthians 2, he tells us that, 'The natural man receiveth not the things of the Spirit of God: for they are foolishness unto him: neither can he know them, because they are spiritually discerned' (verse 14). How then does anyone believe? He says, 'God hath revealed them unto us by his Spirit' (verse 10). And again, 'We have received, not the spirit of the world, but the spirit which is of God; that we might know the things that are freely given to us of God' (verse 12). It is the Spirit who does this work, and it is an effectual work. He does the same thing in each one of us, though there may be minor and unimportant differences in detail. The result is that He produces an identity of belief and of outlook, and especially of hope. In other words, these people are all looking in the same direction. A verse of a hymn sums it up for us:

> *One the object of our journey,*
> *One the faith which never tires,*

> *One the earnest looking forward,*
>   *One the hope our God inspires.*
> *One the gladness of rejoicing*
>   *On the far eternal shore,*
> *Where the one almighty Father*
>   *Reigns in love for evermore.*

'One hope of your calling'! These people have become 'strangers and pilgrims' in this world. They are new men with an entirely new outlook, and they are all looking towards the same eternal home. They have 'one hope of their calling', the blessed hope of the coming of our Lord, the final judgment of sin and evil, the setting up of His eternal kingdom, and their reigning with Him in the glory everlasting. 'One Spirit'! The one work of the one Spirit always leads to 'one hope of your calling'.

II. 'ONE LORD, ONE FAITH, ONE BAPTISM'

First we must emphasize the fact that there is only 'one Lord'. This was the very essence of apostolic preaching. Peter states it unequivocally and boldly when he and John were arraigned before the authorities. 'There is none other name under heaven given among men, whereby we must be saved' (*Acts* 4:12). There is no other! There is no second! You cannot put anybody by His side. He is absolutely unique. He is no mere man, teacher, or prophet. He is the Son of God! He is the Lord of glory who has taken to Himself human nature! 'One Lord – Jesus Christ', and there is no other. Paul puts it thus in a memorable statement: 'For though there be that are

[31]

called gods, whether in heaven or in earth, (as there be gods many, and lords many,) but to us there is but one God, the Father, of whom are all things, and we in him; and one Lord Jesus Christ, by whom are all things, and we by him' (*1 Cor.* 8:5–6). He expresses the same truth again in 1 Timothy 2: 5: 'There is one God, and one mediator'– and only one – 'between God and men, the man Christ Jesus.'

Now, in the matter of Christian unity this is essential. The unity is the unity of those who believe that there is only 'one Lord', and that He is so perfect, and His work so perfect, that He needs no assistance. There is no co-redemptrix such as the Roman Catholics claim the Virgin Mary to be. There is no assistant needed. The Christian does not need the supererogation of the saints, and does not need to pray to them.

There is only one Mediator, and He is enough. He is complete in and of Himself, and nothing must be added to Him and His perfect completed work. The only unity known to the New Testament is that of people who believe this truth. It is an essential part of the definition of the unity. We look to this unique Lord, and we look at no-one but Him. He is the first and the last, the Alpha and the Omega, the beginning and the end; He is the all and in all. 'He that glorieth, let him glory in the Lord.' 'One Lord'!

Paul reminds us also that there is but 'one faith'. What does this mean? This is more difficult. There are those who say that it is a reference to our subjective faith, to our belief, or to the quality of our faith. That is included,

I believe; but it seems to me to stop far short of the real emphasis of the apostle at this point. There is surely an objective element here. Does this mean that we must subscribe to a certain complete and full confession of faith or to a particular creed? It cannot be that, because there have always been differences in such confessions at certain points and with respect to certain details. That is the thing to which we come eventually, as he points out in verse 13. But he says here that there is already this 'one faith'.

What is this one faith? It seems to me that there is only one answer to the question. It is the great essential New Testament message concerning justifying faith. That was the very nerve and centre of apostolic preaching. It is stated perfectly by this same apostle in the words, 'I am not ashamed of the gospel of Christ: for it is the power of God unto salvation to every one that believeth; to the Jew first, and also to the Greek. For therein is the righteousness of God revealed from faith to faith: as it is written, The just shall live by faith' (*Rom.* 1: 16–17). This was the kernel of apostolic preaching, that it is by faith a man is justified, not by the deeds of the law, nor any righteousness of his own.

We have a classic statement of it in Romans 3. Having reminded us that as Christians we are now in a new position, in the words, 'But now the righteousness of God without the law is manifested' (verse 21), Paul goes on to say, 'Being justified freely by his grace through the redemption that is in Christ Jesus: whom God hath set forth to be a propitiation through faith in his blood, to declare his righteousness for the remission of sins that are past, through the forbearance of God; to declare, I say, at this time his righteousness: that he might be just, and the justifier of him which believeth in Jesus. Where is boasting then? It is excluded. By what law? of works? Nay: but by the law of faith. Therefore we conclude that a man is justified by faith without the deeds of the law' (verses 24–27).

That is the great central message of the gospel. It is through this faith in the Lord Jesus Christ and His work that we are justified. That is the meaning of this 'one faith'. It is, of course, the whole argument of the Epistle to the Galatians. This is the gospel, and there is no other gospel, says the apostle. And the gospel is that God justifies the ungodly who believe in Jesus.

This 'one faith' is something that is set over against every other teaching with regard to the way of salvation. It is this 'one faith' over against 'baptismal regeneration'. It is this 'one faith' over against 'transmissible grace'. It is against all notions that we can justify ourselves by works or actions, our own, or those of others. It is the teaching that it is Christ alone who saves, and that we become participants in this salvation through faith. So we have 'one Lord, one faith'.

This brings us to the phrase 'one baptism'. Here again is something which we must look at carefully. I remember reading a comment on this 'one baptism' in a Christian weekly paper. The writer was happy to dismiss it with the words, 'Of course, this means water baptism by immersion.' But, surely, in the whole context we cannot regard this as just a reference to the mode of baptism. You notice that it is put under this heading of 'one Lord'. What is the significance of that? He is the one Lord in whom we believe by faith, and by whom we are saved through faith.

But, furthermore, we have to realize that we are incorporated into Him. That is the apostle's theme at this point. He has been talking about the 'one body', and he will tell us in verse 15 that Christ is the head of this 'one body'. So the obvious interpretation of this 'one baptism' is that it is a reference to our baptism into Christ. Not merely a baptism into His name, because that again calls our attention to the physical act of baptizing, whereas the apostle here is concerned rather with the question of the mystical union which is symbolized by that act.

It seems to me, therefore, that this is a reference to our being baptized into the Lord Jesus Christ. I am suggesting, in other words, that it is just another way of putting what the apostle says in 1 Corinthians 12:13. There he is talking about the 'one body' as he is here in Ephesians 4, and this is how he puts it: 'For by one Spirit are we all baptized into one body, whether we be Jews or Gentiles, whether we be bond or free; and have been all made to drink into one Spirit.'

The unity we have to 'keep' is unity in the 'one Lord'. Faith is the instrument which points us to Him; but furthermore, we are incorporated into Him, we are baptized into Him, we are 'in Christ'. It is exactly the same idea as we found in the second chapter, where Paul says that everything that happens to us happens because of our union with Christ: quickened with him, raised with him, seated with him in the heavenly places.

It is exactly the same teaching as is found in Romans 6: 3–5: 'Know ye not, that so many of us as were baptized into Jesus Christ were baptized into his death? Therefore we are buried with him by baptism into death: that like as Christ was raised up from the dead by the glory of the Father, even so we also should walk in newness of life. For if we have been planted together in the likeness of his death, we shall be also in the likeness of his resurrection.' This is the great and exalted teaching about the union of the believer with the Lord Jesus Christ. Or as it is put in Romans 5 we who were 'in Adam' are now 'in Christ', and we receive all the benefits of His person and of His work. 'One Lord, one faith, one baptism.'

III. 'ONE GOD AND FATHER OF ALL'

The third big assertion is this glorious statement about the Father: 'One God and Father of all, who is above all, and through all, and in you all.' This is the end and the ultimate in the matter of salvation. We do not stop at the Lord Jesus Christ, the Son of God. He came and He died, as Peter reminds us, to 'bring us to God' (*1 Pet.* 3: 18). Here we arrive at the ultimate source of all union, the God, the only God, who has created all things, by whom all things are kept going, the God who planned this great salvation and who sent His Son. We are 'His people'. We all go to Him together and worship Him as 'our Father'. 'This is life eternal,' says our Lord, 'that they might know thee the only true God, and Jesus Christ, whom thou hast sent' (*John* 17:3). The knowledge of God! That is the ultimate goal, the *summum bonum*. There is only one God, there is only one knowledge, and we know Him as 'our Father'.

'Ye have not received the spirit of bondage again to fear; but ye have received the Spirit of adoption, whereby we cry, Abba, Father. The Spirit itself beareth witness with our spirit, that we are the children of God: and if children, then heirs; heirs of God, and joint heirs with Christ' (*Rom.* 8:15–17). This is the thing that makes us one. We are 'children' of the same Father. We know that He has a great inheritance prepared for us. And the unity that obtains among us is the unity of those who are 'joint-heirs with Christ', who are waiting for the final consummation and their entrance into the presence of God. 'Blessed are the pure in heart: for they shall see God' (*Matt.* 5:8). He is over all and 'above all, and through all, and in you all'.

That is the account which the apostle gives of the nature of this unity, and the point that he is making is, of course, that there is no unity unless we are agreed about these things and participating in them. Paul's teaching here is exactly the same as that of our Lord in John 17. Unity is not something which exists, or of which you can speak, in and of itself. It is always the consequence of our belief and acceptance of this great and glorious doctrine of God who has provided in His Son the way of salvation, and who mediates it to us through the operation of the Holy Spirit. That is the basis and the nature of Christian unity. It must never be thought of except in terms of this great background, this essential doctrine.

6. God's Gifts to the Church

We saw in our analysis of the whole section that in verses 7 to 12 the apostle teaches that God has appointed certain means to preserve and to develop this unity. This is of course of great importance, but as our present objective is a limited one we cannot go into it in detail. It is wonderful to realize that, though we are all one in the fundamental sense of which we have been speaking, we are not all identical. To 'every one of us is given grace according to the measure of the gift of Christ'. There is diversity in this great unity, as is illustrated, of course, by the analogy of the body to which Paul has already referred and with which he deals in greater detail in verses 15 and 16.

In verses 8, 9 and 10 the apostle turns aside to indicate how the Lord is in the position of being able to give these gifts according to the measure of His grace. He rejoices in the one who has ascended up on high, and has received gifts which He can then give to men. Who is this? He is the one who 'descended first into the lower parts of the earth'. The whole marvel and miracle of the incarnation is essential to this giving of gifts. It is the one who came from glory, who humbled Himself, and came 'in the likeness of men' and 'of sinful flesh', became a servant, came right down to earth and lived our life and died our death. This is the same one who has 'ascended up far above all heavens, that he might fill all things'. It is He who now dispenses these gifts. Why does He give these gifts? For the sake and the good of His people. 'And he gave some, apostles; and some, prophets; and some, evangelists; and some, pastors and teachers.' What for? They are there for the benefit of the church. He has planned the church and brought her into being, and He has provided these offices and officers in the church 'for the perfecting of the saints'. It is in order that we who have become believers, and are in this 'one body', and sharing in this glorious unity, might be taught and trained.

Verses 13 to 16 deal with the subject of what we are being trained for. Here we are looking at what I described earlier as the ultimate goal: 'Till we all come in the unity of the faith, and of the knowledge of the Son of God, unto a perfect man, unto the measure of the stature of the fulness of Christ.' Then negatively: 'That we henceforth be no more children, tossed to and fro, and carried about with every wind of doctrine, by the sleight of men, and cunning craftiness, whereby they lie in wait to deceive; but speaking the truth in love, may grow up into him in all things, which is the head, even Christ: from whom the whole body fitly joined together and compacted by that which every joint supplieth, according to the effectual working in the measure of every part, maketh increase of the body unto the edifying of itself in love.'

7. The Heart of the Problem

It is at this point that we come to the heart and centre of the common modern misunderstanding. The popular idea is that, having decided to have fellowship together, though we may disagree fundamentally about doctrine, by meeting together, by being kind and friendly to one another, by working and evangelizing together, and by praying together, we eventually can hope to arrive at an agreement even about doctrine. Of course, we must not start with doctrine, because according to the accepted slogan, 'doctrine always divides'. And it is claimed that the verses we are considering teach that. Our object is to show that the teaching here is actually the exact opposite of that.

1. UNITY AND FAITH IN EPHESIANS 4

Notice that in verse 13 the apostle says 'we all': 'Till we all come . . .'. Now that refers to the same people we have already defined, those who have believed and received 'the gospel of salvation'. 'We all', are the people referred to in 1:12–13, the Jews who have received and believed the message, the Gentiles who have done the same thing. In other words, they are the people who have already accepted the doctrine. He says, 'Till we all arrive at the unity of the faith'. The New English Bible has here, 'the unity inherent in our faith', and that is surely right. In other words, you cannot have the unity without the faith.

The question that arises is, Does this allow for present disagreement about doctrine? Does it look forward to an ultimate agreement as the result of our fellowship together? The apostle himself answers the question by telling us that what he is dealing with is the 'perfecting' of something that is already in existence. He is not teaching that we are going to 'arrive' at something which was non-existent before. What he is saying is that what is in existence already is going to grow and develop and ultimately will be perfected. I argue thus because he says in verse 12 that the whole object of providing apostles and prophets and evangelists and pastors and teachers is 'the perfecting of the saints', that they may be useful in ministering to the building up of the body of Christ.

This interpretation may be further substantiated. Paul says, 'Till we all come in the unity of the faith, and of the knowledge of the Son of God.' Now, to translate the word used by the apostle by the word 'knowledge' is quite inadequate. What the apostle wrote was *epignosis*, which means 'full knowledge'. In other words, we already have knowledge, but the function of the officers in the church is to bring us to '*full* knowledge'. In the same way we have faith, and believe the faith, already. What is needed is the 'full' perfection of that. He is not envisaging a gathering of people who differ with regard to basic doctrine but who, through meeting together and through fellowship, may ultimately arrive at the same basic doctrine. That is entirely foreign to what the apostle is saying. He is writing to people who are already one in their doctrine, and one in their knowledge of the Lord Jesus Christ; but it is not perfect, or fully developed, as yet.

Now that, I suggest, is the key to the understanding of this passage. If there were any doubt about it he settles it once and for all by his use of the negative in verse 14: 'That we henceforth be no more children, tossed to and fro, and carried about with every wind of doctrine, by the sleight of men, and cunning craftiness, whereby they lie in wait to deceive.' His desire is that his readers should become adult men, that they should not remain as children. Surely that puts the matter entirely beyond dispute. Even as 'children', incomplete, not fully developed, they are one. They stand as an acorn does in relation to the full-grown oak. The moment we grasp that, we see that the current popular use of this passage is entirely false to the apostle's teaching. He is not hoping or trying to produce agreement; his concern is that the understanding, the agreement, the knowledge, and the faith which they already have should grow and develop into its ultimate completeness and fullness.

II. NEW TESTAMENT TEACHING ON MATURITY

This is teaching which is found very frequently in the New Testament. The apostle Peter realizes that we need to 'grow in grace, and in the knowledge of our Lord and Saviour Jesus Christ' (2 Pet. 3:18), but before we can grow we must be born. It is only a living child who can grow. There can be no growth where there is no life. The very notion of growth and development and perfection presupposes a life already in existence. Exactly the same point is made by Paul at the beginning of 1 Corinthians 3. He complains that the Corinthians are still babes, that he cannot write to them as men because they are not yet in a condition to receive it. But remember, they are already Christians, 'called saints'; they are born again, they have believed in 'Jesus Christ and him crucified'. They are on the one and only foundation already; but that does not mean that they are complete. They need to be taught. This knowledge needs to develop and to grow; there are aspects of it they have not yet understood.

At the end of Hebrews 5 the author makes the same complaint about his readers, that he cannot feed them with 'strong meat' but can give them only 'milk'. He would like to tell them about the wonderful doctrine of Christ as Melchisedec, but he cannot. Yet the life is there: they have believed the truth; they have laid hold of the 'first principles', the elements of the gospel of Christ. The writer's concern is that they should not 'slip away' by believing false teachers. At the same time he wants them to 'go on unto perfection'.

Much the same thought is expressed in 1 Corinthians 13:12: 'Now we see through a glass, darkly; but then face to face: now I know in part; but then shall I know even as also I am known.' The fact that we now see in a glass darkly does not mean that we do not see at all or that we do not see certain things clearly. That statement in no way allows or makes provision for disagreement about the fundamentals of Christianity among Christians. No, what Paul is saying is that all of us who are agreed about these things are only seeing the glorious thing itself as in a glass darkly now, but then we shall see it face to face, in all its fullness; then shall we know even as we are known now. That is precisely the idea we have here. From all these illustrations and parallel passages we see that the apostle is concerned about the development of what is already in existence, rather than about arriving at something which has been hitherto non-existent. There is no question about this.

The foundation is always there, and must be there, that is, 'Jesus Christ, and him crucified' (*1 Cor.* 2:2). It is 'the foundation of the apostles and prophets' (*Eph.* 2:20), their fundamental teaching.

Perhaps the clearest statement of the point which the apostle is making here is found in Philippians 3:10, where he says that his greatest desire is 'that I may know him'. Does he mean by that, that he did not know Him at all, and that he is longing to have a knowledge of Christ? Of course not. What he is saying is this: I do know Him, but I want to know Him much more. I want to have a deeper knowledge. He longs for an 'increase' and for the perfecting of the knowledge he already has.

To put the matter finally beyond dispute we may turn to the paradoxical statement of Philippians 3:12–15. Paul begins, 'Not as though I had already attained, either were already perfect'; and then continues, 'Let us therefore, as many as be perfect, be thus minded' (verse 15). What does he mean?

There is no real contradiction, of course. What he means is that all true Christians already have the knowledge essential to salvation and are perfect in that sense. So he says, 'Let us therefore, as many as be perfect, be thus minded.' Then he goes on to say, 'If in any thing ye be otherwise minded, God shall reveal even this unto you.' There are still aspects of the faith and of the truth which we do not yet know; they will be revealed to us.

As regards the faith we have, and our present position on the foundation, Christ Jesus, there is a sense, therefore, in which we are already perfect. But we must also go

[44]

on to perfection. We have not arrived, have not 'already attained' (verse 12). We are now growing in this knowledge that we have. We are now coming into it. It is because we are in it already that we can grow and develop in and through it.

The apostle Peter teaches the same thing: 'Desire the sincere milk of the word, that ye may grow thereby: if so be ye have tasted that the Lord is gracious' (*1 Pet.* 2:2–3). It is to the people who have 'tasted that the Lord is gracious' that he writes, but they are to go on drinking in the 'milk of the word' in order that they may 'grow thereby'.

In all of these instances the basic assumption as shown by the context is the very opposite of the modern idea of a loose association of people, in disagreement about the elements of the Christian faith, but hoping to reach agreement through fellowship together.

8. The Dangers of False Doctrine

Having clearly established the harmony of our interpretation of the Ephesians passage with other New Testament teaching on Christian growth and development, we return now to verse 14 which is also very important in another way. Paul calls upon his readers to 'be no more children, tossed to and fro, and carried about with every wind of doctrine'. This presupposes just such an essential faith, belief, and knowledge, even in the youngest and most undeveloped Christian, as we have been discussing. How otherwise could these young Christians be exhorted to avoid false teaching and to hate it? Unless they had a knowledge of true teaching by which to test and examine everything else such exhortation would be futile.

We must examine this still more closely, since it is germane to the whole question of unity as it is now being presented to us. The apostle says that we must 'be no more children'. It is interesting to notice what he says about children. What are their characteristics? They are unstable, fickle, ignorant. They like novelty, dislike work, but like play. They dislike being made to think and to reason; they like entertainment and excitement. Children, unfortunately, are very susceptible to showmanship and to that which is plausible and meretricious.

These are their obvious characteristics. But, above all, they are liable to be deceived by that which is false. They are liable, in fact, by their very nature, to be 'carried about with every wind of doctrine' because their understanding is not fully developed. They are 'children'; they have the essential life, but they need to develop, to grow, to be perfected, in order that they may be able more effectively to recognize and guard themselves against that which is false.

What, then, are the characteristics of false teaching? How important it is, in these days when scarcely any standards are recognized, to observe the detailed instruction which the apostle gives about this. 'Sleight of men' is a reference to dice-playing, a reference to deceit, trickery, and cheating. 'Cunning craftiness' is self-explanatory; it depicts the cunning man, the crafty man, the clever man, the subtle man. Paul says that they 'lie in wait'; the picture in the word is of someone following another, tracking him down as a wild animal tracks its prey.

He says that there is an element of deliberate planning, of system, in this false teaching. It is not something haphazard; it is organized and planned; it is laid down as traps are laid down, or as the beast of prey cunningly plans his method of procedure. The apostle sums it all up in Ephesians 6 by using the word 'wiles' – 'the wiles of the devil' (verse 11).

What does he mean? He is dealing with sham and pretence and dishonesty. But what has this to do with the life of the Christian church? There are many instances one could give. One thinks of professors of theology telling their students, 'Now this is the real truth in this matter as discovered by scholarship; but do not preach it yet, the people are not in a position to receive it. You must introduce this carefully and slowly.' This has happened many times during the past hundred years. One thinks, too, of the practice of using such terms as 'Saviour' and 'salvation' while evacuating them of their meaning.

There is also the man who takes an oath of subscription to the articles of a church or who accepts its credal basis but makes mental reservations as he does so. Is not this 'cunning craftiness'? He appears to be taking the oath, but he has his reservations. Or it could apply to the practice of issuing a document but allowing such liberty in its interpretation that those who subscribe to it may hold completely contradictory beliefs as to what the document teaches. It may even amount to being orthodox on paper, and deliberately using phrases to give the impression of orthodoxy, but at the same time attaching a private meaning and significance to the phrases used.

The apostle warns these Ephesians that they are going to be confronted with that kind of thing, that teachers will come along who will be plausible, attractive, nice, ingratiating and entertaining, who will give the impression that they are Christians, but who are not Christians! It is deceitfulness, it is 'cunning craftiness', it is akin to the tactics of the beast of prey. They do it quite deliberately to serve their own ends.

The apostle's point is that if we are to maintain the unity of the church we must beware of that kind of thing and avoid it as we avoid the very plague itself. This surely, therefore, is a most important statement for us at the present time. He is concerned about these young Christians who have 'received' the truth and have 'believed' it and subscribed to it. He is concerned that they should not be deluded, that they should not be led astray by some specious, plausible teaching which masquerades under the name of Christianity, but which is nothing but a lie, and the deceit of Satan himself.

9. Truth and Love

In verse 14 Paul has given us the negative aspect. In the following verse we have his positive teaching: 'Speaking the truth in love, [we] may grow up into him in all things, which is the head, even Christ.' Here again is a much-quoted text, but unfortunately it is not always quoted accurately. Frequently the emphasis is put entirely upon the 'love' and not at all upon the 'truth'. Indeed the position is sometimes such that we are almost told that you cannot have the two together, and that the trouble with evangelicals is that they are so concerned about the truth that they forget the element of love. Let us be honest and admit that the charge may sometimes be true, but let us add that the sin is not one-sided. We all fail in this matter of love and charity.

What the apostle is saying is not that we should avoid doctrine, or minimize doctrine, or suppress doctrine in the interests of love. What he is saying is that we should 'speak the truth in love'. Indeed it is not even just 'speaking the truth'; what he actually says is much stronger. Some say that the translation here should be 'truthing it', that the whole of our life should be in terms of truth. We should have the truth, we should hold the truth, we should walk in the truth, we should speak the truth: 'Truthing it in love.'

In other words you cannot be truly loving unless it is in terms of truth. Let us put the emphasis on the two words. The apostle is not just telling us that we have to be nice and affable and friendly, and that in the interests of fellowship we must be prepared to accommodate, or even suppress, the truth. No! If you truly love a man you want him to know the truth because that alone can save him. But at the same time Paul warns us of the danger of becoming partisan, mere party men.

The truth is to be held in love, and it is to be presented in love. We must not be merely negative or critical, nor must our only concern be to win an argument. So let us put full emphasis upon the two aspects which are mentioned by the apostle. What he is urging is not that we should join together in a 'quest for truth'; he is not talking about searching for truth. He tells us to hold to the truth we have, and represent it and manifest it in the whole of our life, and especially in our speech, in a loving manner.

In other words, we must always contend for the truth in the right spirit. Not in a party spirit, but with a compassionate desire that men and women should come to know this glorious God who is over all, this 'one Lord' who bought us even at the cost of His own precious blood, and the gracious operations and fellowship of the Holy Spirit. And if we hold this doctrine truly, surely it is something which will in and of itself compel us to preach and to present this truth in such a spirit of love.

10. Summary

Let me now attempt to summarize the apostle's teaching in this chapter. The only unity of which this passage speaks is an already existing spiritual unity, which then expresses itself externally. Certain things are essential to it. First and foremost, a fundamental spiritual experience of regeneration or rebirth produced by the Holy Spirit. Unity is never considered except in terms of this 'new nature' and 'new life', which express themselves always in a belief of certain fundamental truths: the 'word' or 'words' of which our Lord speaks in John 17; the 'teaching' or 'doctrine' of which the apostle speaks in Ephesians.

What are these truths? That man is lost and helpless and hopeless because of sin and the Fall. That the Lord Jesus Christ, who is the Son of God, saves us by His perfect life of obedience to the law and by His death, which was the result of His bearing our guilt and the punishment meted out upon it by the law of God. That salvation becomes ours by faith alone; it is apart from any works or any merit in ourselves, and solely as the result of God calling us effectually by His Spirit. That is the faith, without which there is no unity.

Now this is not the whole or the fullness of truth; much more remains for us to grasp and to learn. Otherwise these New Testament Epistles would never have been written. The new-born babe in Christ has not a full understanding; he needs to grow, he needs to be instructed, he needs to be warned and guarded. Hence, again, the New Testament Epistles, and hence the offices appointed in the church. There are many things about which this babe may even be wrong for the time being, or at any rate he may be muddled and confused in his understanding of them.

I emphasize again that he possesses the essential truth, without which there is no salvation at all; but having that he may be very unclear about many other matters. For instance, he may be Calvinistic or Arminian in his understanding of what we may call the mechanism of salvation; but that does not mean that he has not the essential truth. He may know nothing about the doctrine of the final perseverance of the saints; he may be very lacking in his understanding of the doctrine of the union of the believer with Christ; he may be very confused about a good deal of prophetic teaching, and uncertain about some aspects of the sacrament of baptism and about the final glorious hope.

But though all that may be true of him, he nevertheless is a 'child', he is born again of the Spirit. He has received this fundamental message of salvation, the only way of salvation through the Lord Jesus Christ and His work. He needs to grow in his understanding of the many things of which he is at present relatively ignorant, but such matters are not essential to salvation. They are a part of this perfecting, this full knowledge, at which we shall arrive only when we are in the glory itself.

My contention is that the teaching of the New Testament is quite clear about this, that there is an absolute foundation, an irreducible minimum, without which the term 'Christian' is meaningless, and without subscribing to which a man is not a Christian. That is 'the foundation of the apostles and prophets': the doctrine concerning 'Jesus Christ, and him crucified', and justification by faith only. The passages we have considered teach that apart from that there is no such thing as fellowship, no basis of unity at all.

How easy it is to say, Well, it does not matter how much we disagree, let us pray together. But the question arises at once, How does one pray? One man says that he can turn to God whenever he likes, that he has only to sit down and relax, and he is already listening to God and talking to God. The other says that there is only one way of entry into 'the holiest of all', and that is 'by the blood of Jesus'. How can those two men pray together? True fellowship in prayer is not possible unless we are clear as to the way of access into the presence of God. That is why this is so constantly repeated in the New Testament. For instance, Paul says in Romans 5: 1–2: 'Therefore being justified by faith, we have peace with God through our Lord Jesus Christ: by whom also we have access by faith into this grace wherein we stand.' We have no such access without Him. But the other man claims that he has, that a man can pray to God apart from the Lord Jesus Christ, and apart from the influence and the work of the Holy Spirit. What is the point of talking about unity in prayer when it is clearly impossible unless we are agreed as to how one prays?

In the same way the idea that you can evangelize together without bringing doctrine into it is surely the height of folly. If you call upon men to come to Christ certain questions at once inevitably arise: Who is He? Why should one come to Him? How does one come to Him? Why is He called the Saviour? How does He save? From what does He save?

In other words the teaching is that there is no fellowship among people who are not agreed about the 'one Spirit . . . one Lord, one faith, one baptism, one God . . . who is over all'. There is no real fellowship and unity in a group of people where some believe in the wrath of God against sin and that it has already been 'revealed from heaven' (*Rom.* 1:18), and others not only do not believe in the wrath of God at all, but say that it is almost blasphemous to teach such a thing and that they cannot believe in a God who is capable of wrath. Fellowship exists only among those who believe, as the result of the operation of the Holy Spirit, these essential truths concerning man's lost estate, that we are all 'by nature the children of wrath' (*Eph.* 2:3), and the action of God in Christ Jesus for our salvation and restoration. There is no fellowship between people who believe that and those who believe something else, which they may call a gospel but which, as Paul tells the Galatians, is not a gospel (*Gal.* 1:6–7).

How ridiculous it is to suggest that there can be fellowship and unity between those who believe that they are saved and have access into God's presence solely because in His great love He made His own Son 'to be sin for us' (*2 Cor.* 5:21) and spared Him not 'but delivered him up for us all' (*Rom.* 8:32), and those who believe that the death of Christ was a great tragedy, but that God forgives us even that, and that ultimately we save ourselves by our obedience, our good works, and our practice of religion.

Those are the conclusions to which we are driven by our examination of the two passages which are so frequently quoted today. They agree entirely with each other; they say precisely the same thing. But let us turn now to look at some of the supporting evidence elsewhere in the New Testament. We shall soon find that this is not some isolated emphasis.

4

New Testament Corroboration

1. Causes of Disunity

The New Testament teaches that certain things break this unity. What are they? One is that people, instead of looking at Christ, tend to form factions around men and say, as they did at Corinth, 'I am of Paul; and I of Apollos; and I of Cephas.' The question Paul puts to such people is, Have you been baptized into any of these? He answers by reminding them that they have been baptized into Christ alone and that He cannot be divided (*1 Cor.* 1:10–16). The moment you take your eyes off Him and look at anybody else you are already causing a disturbance in this unity and threatening to disrupt it.

Still more important is false teaching. What does this include? Among other things, philosophy, or 'the wisdom of this world'. Paul was terrified, as he tells us in 1 Corinthians 1:17, 'lest the cross of Christ should be made of none effect' through philosophy, through turning it into a notion and an idea instead of believing the stark reality of the fact of what happened there, that God was making 'him to be sin for us, who knew no sin' (*2 Cor.* 5:21), that God was smiting Him with the stripes that we deserve. The apostle foresees the danger of philosophizing or turning the cross into nothing more than a beautiful picture. He says that this destroys the unity completely. The same idea is taught in Colossians 2, where he warns against substituting philosophy, this same wisdom of men, for the facts reported in the gospel and the true meaning of those facts.

John says the same thing in his First Epistle with regard to the antichrist. The antichrists he exposed were those who denied the reality of the incarnation and the work of Christ. Some denied that He had really come in the body and said that He had but a phantom body, and so on. Others denied His deity and regarded Him as but a man. These are the things that cause division because they all interfere with the doctrine concerning the one Spirit, the one Lord, the one Father, and all that is involved in the content of the doctrine.

Others who cause division are those who fall back upon 'the works of the law'. Those were the people who in the early church said that you must be circumcised, that you must keep the law in addition to believing in Christ. That was the heresy which Paul had to deal with in his letter to the Galatians. It is the theme likewise of the Epistle to the Hebrews. Those people did not realize as they should have done that Christ is pre-eminent and all-sufficient, and they were beginning to look back to the old Jewish religion. Those are the people who caused disunity. These Judaizers were obviously in the mind of the apostle as he wrote the third chapter of the Epistle to the Philippians. He has them in mind also in writing 1 Timothy 1.

These people always want to go back under the law, and are ever ready to rely on 'endless genealogies' and other things for their salvation. The apostle's teaching is that the law is all right when it does its own work, but that it is never a means of salvation. Neither law nor angels nor any other agency can save. There is but one message of salvation: 'This is a faithful saying, and worthy of all acceptation, that Christ Jesus came into the world to save sinners' (*1 Tim.* 1: 15). To suggest anything else or to modify that is to cause division.

Then, of course, any attempt to add to Christ and His work has the same effect. Was not that the chief point under discussion in the council at Jerusalem reported in Acts 15? The decision was that no yoke of law must be put upon Christians, that no addition must be made, that Christ is sufficient. The same thing in a different form is dealt with in Colossians, where the apostle denounces talk about intermediaries, and all the various angels and hierarchies that were supposed to come between man and God, because they are not necessary. He denounces such teaching because it causes disunity. Why, and how?

Because it interferes with the fundamental faith and belief which makes a man a Christian at all.

The third group of things which cause disunity includes everything that exalts self and not Christ. Some in the early church were glorying in their spiritual gifts. But they are reprimanded because that again detracts from Him, takes our eyes off Him, and all the truth as it is in Christ Jesus. Anything that has that effect is always disruptive. Self leads to jealousy and rivalry and disputation and so Christ is 'divided'.

2. Doctrine Can Be Defined

Let us now look at it positively. The New Testament everywhere insists upon true doctrine. I emphasize this because, as we have seen, the whole tendency today is to discourage talk about doctrine and to urge that we work together, pray together, and evangelize together, because 'doctrine divides'. Doctrine is being discounted in the interests of supposed unity. The fact is, however, that there is no unity apart from truth and doctrine, and it is departure from this that causes division and breaks unity.

The first thing the New Testament emphasizes is that doctrine can be defined. If this were not so Paul would never have written his Epistle to the Romans. He had been unable to visit them, so he writes to them a summary of his teaching. It is a great doctrinal statement in which the cardinal doctrines of justification, atonement, union with Christ, assurance, the final perseverance of the saints, and so on, are set forth. Let us remind ourselves again of 1 Corinthians 3:11: 'Other foundation can no man lay than that is laid.' The apostle had already laid it: Jesus Christ and Him crucified; there is no other. That is an absolute. What is the purpose of 1 Corinthians 15? Is it not to say just this: that belief or disbelief in the literal physical resurrection is not an immaterial or unimportant point? The apostle says that it is as important as this, that if it had not happened, 'then is our preaching vain, and your faith is also vain . . . ye are yet in your sins' (verses 14, 17).

But the whole tendency today is to say that it does not matter whether a man believes in the literal physical resurrection or not. The apostle Paul says that it is an absolute and that there is no gospel apart from it: 'Ye are yet in your sins'!

The same argument is found in 2 Timothy 2. Nowhere, perhaps, is it stated more clearly than in the first chapter of the Epistle to the Galatians. He 'marvels' that they are so soon turned away from the gospel which he had preached to them: 'I marvel that ye are so soon removed from him that called you into the grace of Christ unto another gospel: which is not another . . .' (*Gal.* 1:6–7). How can he say that if you cannot define the gospel?

But that is far removed from the modern attitude, and the way in which the subject of unity is being presented today. We are told that the Christian faith cannot be stated in propositions, that it is something mystical which cannot be analysed or put down in a series of definitions stating what is right and what is wrong. By saying that, they are not only running counter to the practice of the church in the early centuries when she drew up her creeds and confessions of faith; they are also denying the teaching of the New Testament itself which maintains that truth can be so defined that you can say that a man has departed from it. For how can you say that a man has departed from something if you do not know what the thing itself is? The whole presupposition is that it can be defined and described accurately.

Nothing is so interesting as to contrast the ecumenical councils of the first centuries of the Christian era with the World Council of Churches today. The great concern of the former was doctrine: definition of doctrine and denunciation of error and heresy. The chief characteristic of the modern movement is doctrinal indifferentism and the exaltation of a spirit of inclusivism and practical co-operation.

But the apostle goes even further than that. He says to the Philippians, 'Brethren, be followers together of me' (*Phil.* 3:17). He does not hesitate to put it like that. He appeals to them to follow him and his teaching and example. That follows from what he has already said: 'Nevertheless, whereto we have already attained, let us walk by the same rule, let us mind the same thing' (verse 16). They were to think the same thing, and to go on preaching and teaching the same thing.

In 2 Timothy 2:8 he talks about 'my gospel'. He is contrasting it with 'other gospels'. He is not saying what I once remember reading in a sermon on this text: 'The important thing is that you should have an experience, that you should be able to say "my gospel". Of course, it may not be the other man's gospel, but the thing is, can you say "my gospel"?' According to that interpretation the important thing is to have an experience, to be able to say that something has happened to you. The precise cause of the experience is regarded as being unimportant.

But the apostle, surely, is teaching the exact opposite of that. He is saying that his gospel alone is the true gospel, not because it was his, or because of what it had done for him, but because of what God had done in Christ. The context in which he makes his statement is the false teaching of others. He says, 'Remember that Jesus Christ of the seed of David was raised from the dead according to my gospel.' There were other teachers who said that 'the resurrection is past already', and they were overthrowing 'the faith of some' (verse 18). Do not listen to them, he says. The gospel that he, Paul, preached was the only true gospel, and any teaching that contradicted it was a lie.

In other words, he not only defines it, and says that it can be defined, but he says, This is it, and every other is wrong. The same truth emerges in Hebrews 4:14–16: 'Seeing then that we have a great high priest, that is passed into the heavens, Jesus the Son of God, let us hold fast our profession' – our confession, the faith which we believe concerning Him – 'Jesus the Son of God'.

The remedy for the unhappiness of those Hebrew Christians was not to cultivate a vague general spirit of fellowship, but to hold fast the cardinal doctrines. What are they? The doctrine of the person of Christ. The incarnation. Christ as our high priest who has offered His own blood as an atonement for sins, as the writer goes on to explain in chapters 7 to 10. That is the only way in which we can enter into the 'rest' that God has provided for His people. We must know the doctrine and hold on to it and reject all false teaching. It is also the only way in which we can approach 'boldly unto the throne of grace, that we may obtain mercy, and find grace to help in time of need'.

Everywhere in the New Testament, as we have seen, there is an insistence upon true doctrine in contra-distinction to false doctrine. That is only possible because doctrine can be defined and stated in terms and propos-itions. We have an objective standard by which we can test ourselves and others.

3. The New Testament Condemns False Teaching

This becomes even clearer when we note the way in which false teaching is denounced in the New Testament, and the language which is used with regard to false teachers.

In particular, observe the way in which our Lord Himself does this. For the whole climate of opinion today is utterly opposed to this. I find it amusing to notice in the reviews of books that a point which is almost always emphasized is whether the writer has been entirely positive or not. We must never be negative; we must never be critical of other views. That is regarded as sub-Christian. It is the spirit that matters. So we must never criticize, still less must we denounce anything. Views which are totally divergent are to be regarded as valuable 'insights' which point in the direction of truth.

The fact is, of course, that in our misunderstanding of the New Testament and its teaching we are exalting a kind of niceness and politeness, which are not to be found there, not even in the Lord Jesus Christ Himself. Look, for instance, at what He says in Matthew 7:15–27. He says that there are false teachers whom He can compare only to 'wolves in sheep's clothing'. No severer castigation than that can be imagined. He is referring to men who themselves are deniers of the truth but who give the impression that they are preaching it. He warns us against them. They are 'false prophets', 'false teachers', people who claim that they belong to Him and say, Lord, Lord, have we not done this, that and the other in thy name? He says that they are liars and that, at the great day of judgment, He will say to them, 'I never knew you'! They have never been His at all. One cannot imagine any stronger teaching than that.

Or take what He teaches in Matthew 24:24–26. There He issues a most important warning to His followers and to all Christian people throughout the centuries: 'For there shall arise false Christs, and false prophets, and shall shew great signs and wonders; insomuch that, if it were possible, they shall deceive the very elect. Behold,

I have told you before. Wherefore if they shall say unto you, Behold, he is in the desert; go not forth: behold, he is in the secret chambers; believe it not.' Here He is warning us against false and deceitful teachers. The language once again is very strong.

We have already seen the same thing in Ephesians 4. Here is the great apostle, filled with the spirit of love, and, let us remember, 'speaking the truth in love'; but the language he uses, as we have seen, is, 'Be no more children, tossed to and fro, and carried about with every wind of doctrine, by the sleight of men, and cunning craftiness . . .'.

That is 'speaking the truth in love'. It includes denouncing these false teachers in the church and making clear the sort of people they are and the kind of thing they do. He describes them as predatory beasts lying in wait 'to deceive'. To speak the truth in love includes a clear exposition of error, and everything that can be harmful to 'babes in Christ'.

Even stronger language is used by the apostle in his farewell address to the elders of the church at Ephesus: 'Take heed therefore unto yourselves, and to all the flock, over the which the Holy Ghost hath made you overseers, to feed the church of God, which he hath purchased with his own blood. For I know this, that after my departing shall grievous wolves enter in among you, not sparing the flock. Also of your own selves shall men arise, speaking perverse things, to draw away disciples after them. Therefore watch, and remember, that by the space of three years I ceased not to warn every one night and day with tears'

(*Acts* 20:28–31). That is the language! 'Wolves'! 'Grievous wolves'!

In 2 Corinthians 11:13–15 he calls them 'false apostles' who are like the devil, who 'himself is transformed into an angel of light'. In Galatians 1:8 he says, 'Though we, or an angel from heaven, preach any other gospel unto you . . . let him be *anathema*', that is, 'let him be accursed'.

All that comes under the heading of 'speaking the truth in love'. Why is such speech abominated today and regarded as sub-Christian? Because the notion of truth as something which can be defined has gone, and we are replacing it by a flabby, sentimental notion of unity and of fellowship.

In Philippians 3:18–19 the apostle writes, 'For many walk, of whom I have told you often, and now tell you even weeping, that they are the enemies of the cross of Christ: whose end is destruction, whose God is their belly, and whose glory is in their shame, who mind earthly things.' Such people were in the church and represented themselves as teachers of the truth of the gospel, but the apostle does not hesitate to denounce them as 'enemies of the cross of Christ'. Why? Because they were denying this essential doctrine at some point.

We must speak the truth in love about such people in order that the 'children' in the faith may be protected from their nefarious influence. The terms used about such people are extraordinary in their strength and variation. Paul talks about 'philosophy and vain deceit'; 'the traditions of men' (*Col.* 2:8); 'profane and vain babblings' (*1 Tim.* 6:20); words which 'will eat as doth a canker [cancer]' (*2 Tim.* 2:17). The apostle Peter in equally strong terms speaks of 'wells without water' (*2 Pet.* 2:17). They appear to have something but in reality have nothing. What is in their gospel, what is its content? They stand and talk glibly about love; but what is the love of which they are speaking? Where is their salvation? What is the meaning of the terms which they are employing?

Look also at the language used by Jude. Look at the language used in the letters to the churches in Revelation 2 and 3. The New Testament talks about people being carried away with 'strong delusion', and people believing 'a lie' (*2 Thess.* 2: 11). The false prophets are referred to as 'dogs', as those who teach and speak 'damnable heresies', whose ways are pernicious and who are 'liars'. It refers to false teaching as a canker, a cancer that eats away at the vitals of life. That is New Testament teaching. But all that is abominated today and is regarded as being a complete denial of the spirit of love and of fellowship, indeed of the spirit of Christ.

In other words, this modern teaching about unity has departed so far from the New Testament that it dislikes any polemical element at all in the preaching and the teaching of the truth. As I have said, we are told that we must never be negative, that we should always be positive. The man who is admired is the man who says, I am not a controversialist, I am simply a preacher of the gospel! Some evangelists and others who are evangelical in their own views are praised by those who are very liberal in their theology on the grounds that they do not 'attack' liberalism and modernism. That is what is admired. Any polemical element is regarded as a negation of the Christian spirit. We must never criticize; we must always be kind and friendly. I agree that we must always be kind and friendly, we must always 'speak the truth in *love*'. But we must always 'speak the *truth* in love'. We must, as the New Testament itself does, 'contend for the faith'. We must expose error and denounce it and not be men-pleasers only. The New Testament is full of that, as I have just proved.

That is what was done at the time of the Protestant Reformation. That is what is always done in times of revival and renewal because at such times there is a return to the New Testament. Error is unmasked, exposed, and denounced. It was done, likewise, in the time of the Puritans. Let us remember, in these days when 'niceness' and 'friendliness' and 'fellowship' are exalted to the supreme position and at the expense of truth, that the exhortation addressed to the New Testament teachers and believers was not that they should be ready to agree with anything for the sake of unity and fellowship.

The exhortation addressed to them in 1 Corinthians 16:13–14 is: 'Watch ye, stand fast in the faith, quit you like men, be strong. Let all your things be done with charity.' We are to be men, we are to be strong, we are to stand fast in the faith which we have believed. We are to know that we have a foundation beneath our feet and we must know what it is. We are not to be riding on clouds; we are not to be in the air; we are to be 'standing fast' on a solid recognizable, definable foundation. We are exhorted to 'earnestly contend for the faith' (*Jude* 3).

In 2 John we are told that we are not to receive into our house, or to 'bid God speed' to, a false teacher, and that to do so is to be 'partaker of his evil deeds' (verses 10–11).

In 2 Thessalonians 2:15 the apostle uses these words, 'Therefore, brethren, stand fast, and hold the traditions which ye have been taught, whether by word, or our epistle.' Traditions taught by word and in writing! Something definable, something concrete, something clear, something which is unmistakable. That was written to people such as the Thessalonians, to young Christians in the faith. And we are to contend for it earnestly, with all our might and power.

In Titus 3:10–11, the apostle sums it all up again in a most important statement: 'A man that is an heretick after the first and second admonition reject; knowing that he that is such is subverted, and sinneth, being condemned of himself.' We are not to be 'nice and friendly' to him. If he persists in being a heretic after the first and second admonition, we are to reject him. He is a danger to the church and we must put him out. That is the plain and explicit teaching of the New Testament everywhere.

All this, of course, is quite inevitable in view of the nature of the truth concerning salvation, and the nature of the unity that obtains in the church. But it is far removed from the popular teaching of today which not only tolerates the doctrine of men who deny the plain New Testament teaching concerning our Lord's Person and work, but even exalts them and praises them as outstanding Christians worthy of the emulation of young believers.

5

Conclusions

It may be helpful to summarize and list the conclusions we have arrived at.

1. *Unity must never be isolated,* or regarded as something in and of itself.

2. It is equally clear that *the question of unity must never be put first.* We must never start with it, always bearing in mind the order stated so clearly in Acts 2:42, where fellowship follows doctrine: 'They continued stedfastly in the apostles' doctrine and fellowship, and in breaking of bread, and in prayers.' That, as we have seen, is precisely the order in which they are placed both in John 17 and in Ephesians 4. The present tendency to discount and to depreciate doctrine in the interests of unity is simply a denial and a violation of plain New Testament teaching.

3. *We must never start with the visible church or with an institution, but rather with the truth,* which alone creates unity. Failure to realize this point was surely the main trouble with the Jews at the time when our Lord was in this world. It is dealt with in the preaching of John the Baptist, when he said, 'Bring forth therefore fruits worthy of repentance, and begin not to say within yourselves, We have Abraham to our father: for I say unto you, That God is able of these stones to raise up children unto Abraham' (*Luke* 3:8).

Our Lord teaches the same thing in John 8:32–34. The Jews had objected to His saying, 'The truth shall make you free', their argument being that they were Abraham's seed, and were never in bondage to any man. He draws attention to their rejection of His Word and their attempts to kill Him, and concludes: 'If ye were Abraham's children, ye would do the works of Abraham . . . Ye do the deeds of your father . . . Ye are of your father the devil' (*John* 8:39, 41, 44). Their fatal assumption was that the fact that they were Jews guaranteed of necessity their salvation, that membership of the nation meant that they were truly children of God. As John the Baptist indicated, the notion was entirely mechanical; God could produce such people out of stones.

The apostle Paul also deals with this confusion when he says, in writing to the Romans: 'For he is not a Jew, which is one outwardly; neither is that circumcision, which is outward in the flesh: but he is a Jew, which is one inwardly; and circumcision is that of the heart, in the spirit, and not in the letter; whose praise is not of men, but of

God' (*Rom.* 2:28, 29). He repeats this when he says, 'For they are not all Israel, which are of Israel' (*Rom.* 9:6). This is further enforced by the statement, 'Know ye therefore that they which are of faith, the same are the children of Abraham' (*Gal.* 3:7). And also, 'And if ye be Christ's, then are ye Abraham's seed, and heirs according to the promise' (*Gal.* 3:29).

The same mistake of starting with the visible institution rather than with truth was also made at the time of the Reformation. What Luther was enabled to see, and what accounted for his courageous stand, was this self-same point. He refused to be bound by that mighty institution, the Roman Catholic Church, with her long centuries of history. Having been liberated by the truth of justification by faith he saw clearly that truth must always come first. It must come before institutions and traditions, and everything. Every institution – even the church – must be judged by the Word of truth. The invisible church is more important than the visible Church, and loyalty to the former may involve either expulsion or separation from the latter, and the formation of a new visible church.

4. *The starting point in considering the question of unity must always be regeneration and belief of the truth.* Nothing else produces unity, and, as we have seen clearly, it is impossible apart from this.

5. *An appearance or a façade of unity based on anything else, and at the expense of these two criteria, or ignoring them, is clearly a fraud and a lie.* People are not one, nor in a state

of unity, who disagree about fundamental questions such as, (i) whether we submit ourselves utterly to revealed truth or rely ultimately upon our reason and human thinking; (ii) the historic Fall, and man's present state and condition in sin, under the wrath of God, and in complete helplessness and hopelessness as regards salvation; and (iii) the Person of our Lord Jesus Christ and the utter, absolute necessity, and sole sufficiency, of His substitutionary atoning work for sinners. To give the impression that they are one simply because of a common outward organization is not only to mislead the world which is outside the church but to be guilty of a lie.

6. *To do anything which supports or encourages such an impression or appearance of unity is surely dishonest and sinful.* Truth and untruth cannot be reconciled, and the difference between them cannot be patched over. Error is always to be exposed and denounced for truth's sake, and also, as we have seen, for the sake of babes in Christ. This is also important from the standpoint of the prayer in John 17:21, 'That the world may believe that thou hast sent me'. Nothing so surely drives the world away from the truth as uncertainty or confusion in the church with respect to the content of her message.

That is undoubtedly the main cause of the present declension in religion. The world will not be impressed by a mere coming together in externals while there is central disagreement about the fundamentals of the faith. It will interpret it as an attempt on the part of church authorities to save their institution in much the same way as it sees business men forming combines and amalgam-ations with the same object and intention. The question the world is still asking is, What is Christianity? What is your teaching? Have you anything authoritative and powerful to offer us? It is interested in this rather than in organizational matters, and rightly so. It is also ready to respond to it.

7. *To regard a church, or a council of churches, as a forum in which fundamental matters can be debated and discussed, or as an opportunity for witness-bearing, is sheer confusion and muddled thinking.* There is to be no discussion about 'the foundation', as we have seen. If men do not accept that, they are not brethren and we can have no dialogue with them. We are to preach to such and to evangelize them. Discussion takes place only among brethren who share the same life and subscribe to the same essential truth. It is right and good that brethren should discuss together matters which are not essential to salvation and about which there is, and always has been, and probably always will be, legitimate difference of opinion. We can do no better at that point than quote the old adage, 'In things essential unity, in things indifferent liberty, in all things charity.'

Before there can be any real discussion and dialogue and exchange there must be agreement concerning primary and fundamental matters. Without the accept-ance of certain axioms and propositions in geometry, for example, it is idle to attempt to solve any problem. If certain people refuse to accept the axioms, and are constantly querying and disputing them, clearly there is no point of contact between them and those who do accept them. It is precisely the same in the realm of the church. Those who question and query, let alone deny, the great cardinal truths that have been accepted throughout the centuries do not belong to the church, and to regard them as brethren is to betray the truth. As we have already reminded ourselves, the apostle Paul tells us clearly what our attitude to them should be: 'A man that is an heretick after the first and second admonition reject' (*Titus* 3:10). They are to be regarded as unbelievers who need to be called to repentance and acceptance of the truth as it is in Christ Jesus. To give the impression that they are Christians with whom other Christians disagree about certain matters is to confuse the genuine seeker and enquirer who is outside. But such is the position prevailing today. It is based upon a failure to understand the nature of the New Testament church which is 'the pillar and ground of the truth' (*1 Tim.* 3:15).

In the same way it is a sheer waste of time to discuss or debate the implications of Christianity with people who are not agreed as to what Christianity is. Failure to realize this constitutes the very essence of the modern confusion.

8. *Unity must obviously never be thought of primarily in numerical terms,* but always in terms of life. Nothing is so opposed to the biblical teaching as the modern idea that numbers and powerful organization alone count. It is the very opposite of the great biblical doctrine of 'the

remnant', stated, for instance, so perfectly by Jonathan to his armour-bearer as they alone faced the hosts of the Philistines, in the words: 'Come, and let us go over unto the garrison of these uncircumcised: it may be that the LORD will work for us: for there is no restraint to the LORD to save by many or by few' (*1 Sam.* 14:6). Still more strikingly, perhaps, is it taught in the incident of Gideon and the Midianites, where we read of God reducing the army of Israel from thirty-two thousand to three hundred as a preliminary to victory (*Judg.* 7).

God has done His greatest work throughout the centuries through remnants, often even through individuals. Why is it that we forget Micaiah the son of Imlah, and Jeremiah, and Amos, John the Baptist, the mere twelve disciples; and Martin Luther, standing alone, defying some twelve centuries of tradition and all the power of a mighty church? This is not to advocate smallness or exclusiveness as if they had some inherent merit; but it is to suggest that the modern slavish attitude to bigness and organization cuts right across a central biblical emphasis. Indeed it suggests ignorance of, and lack of faith in, the power of the Holy Spirit.

9. *The greatest need of the hour is a new baptism and outpouring of the Holy Spirit in renewal and revival.* Nothing else throughout the centuries has ever given the church true authority and made her and her message mighty.

But what right have we to pray for this, or to expect that He will honour or bless anything but the truth that He Himself enabled the authors of the Old Testament and the New Testament to write? To ask Him to do so is not only near blasphemy but also the height of folly. Reformation and revival go together and cannot be separated. He is the Spirit of truth, and He will honour nothing but the truth. The ultimate question facing us these days is whether our faith is in men and their power to organize, or in the truth of God in Christ Jesus and the power of the Holy Spirit. Let me put it another way: Are we primarily concerned about the size of the church or the purity of the church, both in doctrine and in life?

Indeed, finally it comes to this: Is our view of the church *Roman Catholic* (inclusivist, organizational, institutional, and hierarchical) or *Reformed*, emphasizing the universal priesthood of all believers and the need for keeping the church herself constantly under the judgment of the Word?

OTHER TITLES BY OR ABOUT
DR MARTYN LLOYD-JONES
AVAILABLE FROM THE
BANNER OF TRUTH
TRUST

ROMANS SERIES:
The Gospel of God (1:1–32)
ISBN 0 85151 467 7, 408 pp.
The Righteous Judgment of God (2:1–3:20)
ISBN 0 85151 545 2, 240 pp.
Atonement and Justification (3:20–4:25)
ISBN 0 85151 034 5, 272 pp.
Assurance (5:1–21)
ISBN 0 85151 050 7, 384 pp.
The New Man (6:1–23)
ISBN 0 85151 158 9, 328 pp.
The Law (7:1–8:4)
ISBN 0 85151 180 5, 372 pp.
The Sons of God (8:5–17)
ISBN 0 85151 207 0, 400 pp.
Final Perseverance (8:17–39)
ISBN 0 85151 231 3, 460 pp.
God's Sovereign Purpose (9:1–33)
ISBN 0 85151 579 7, 344 pp.
Saving Faith (10:1–21)
ISBN 0 85151 737 4, 411 pp.
To God's Glory (11:1–36)
ISBN 0 85151 748 X, 304 pp.
Christian Conduct (12:1–21)
ISBN 0 85151 794 3, 528 pp.
Life in Two Kingdoms (13:1–14)
ISBN 0 85151 824 9, 336 pp.
Liberty and Conscience (14:1–17)
ISBN 0 85151 849 4, 288 pp.

'Dr Lloyd-Jones is a great biblical theologian, but the reader will be impressed afresh by the strong experimental note in his theology.'

Evangelical Quarterly

'It is solid fare that is presented, but with passion and fervour, with simplicity and clarity.'

Expository Times

'The didactic style that proves so attractive in his pulpit utterances is equally effective in the written page.'

Free Church of Scotland Monthly Record

EPHESIANS SERIES:
God's Ultimate Purpose (1:1–23)
ISBN 0 85151 272 0, 448 pp.
God's Way of Reconciliation (2:1–22)
ISBN 0 85151 299 2, 480 pp.
The Unsearchable Riches of Christ (3:1–21)
ISBN 0 85151 293 3, 320 pp.
Christian Unity (4:1–16)
ISBN 0 85151 312 3, 280 pp.
Darkness and Light (4:17–5:17)
ISBN 0 85151 343 3, 464 pp.
Life in the Spirit (5:18–6:9)
ISBN 0 85151 194 5, 372 pp.
The Christian Warfare (6:10–13)
ISBN 0 85151 243 7, 376 pp.
The Christian Soldier (6:10–20)
ISBN 0 85151 258 5, 368 pp.

(Not available in the USA)

'Characteristically rich in insight, inspiration and interpretation, reflecting his long years of preaching and pastoral experience . . . Even in printed form these sermons reveal the authority of the man who preached them and the greater authority of his message.'

Church of England Newspaper

'Good old-fashioned theological preaching of this kind is a healthy antidote to the superficiality of many modern sermons.'

Scottish Journal of Theology

'If you have grown weak on shallow teaching and fuzzy application, this work will provide strength for the spiritual muscles and courage for the struggle.'

Moody Monthly

ACTS SERIES:
Authentic Christianity, Vol. 1 (1–3)
ISBN 0 85151 776 5, 336 pp.
Authentic Christianity, Vol. 2 (4–5)
ISBN 0 85151 807 9, 336 pp.
Authentic Christianity, Vol. 3 (5–6)
ISBN 0 85151 832 X, 352 pp.

'The style is crystal clear. The content is thoroughly evangelistic. The glory of the gospel shines forth on every page. I thoroughly commend it, truly Dr Lloyd-Jones at his best.'

Evangelical Times

2 PETER
ISBN 0 85151 379 4
272 pp. Cloth-bound; and
ISBN 0 85151 771 4
272 pp. Paperback

'A masterly example of the kind of expository preaching in popular vein that can result in the building up of a congregation in the Christian faith.'

Reformed Theological Review

'A model for preaching and . . . a storehouse of spiritual benefit.'

Ministry

EVANGELISTIC SERMONS
AT ABERAVON
ISBN 0 85151 362 X
308 pp. Large Paperback

'Early examples of that "logic-on-fire" which the author desired and commended to others. To me their abiding value lies in the intense seriousness of the preacher. They are worlds apart from the triviality of so much evangelism today.'

Dick Lucas in *The Churchman*

OLD TESTAMENT
EVANGELISTIC SERMONS
ISBN 0 85151 683 1
304 pp. Cloth-bound

'It is vintage wine indeed, and one could have wished for a volume twice the size. Can we expect more?'

Evangelical Presbyterian

'Nearly fifty years on, and the words are in cold print, yet they fire the soul! And surely that is why the book has been published . . . this book may help us to see how a greater mind than ours avoided the distractions and kept to the one great question . . . buy it! You will not be disappointed.'

Evangelical Action

KNOWING THE TIMES
Addresses delivered on Various Occasions
1942–1977
ISBN 0 85151 556 8
400 pp. Case-bound

'This is a most significant book . . . a challenge to return to Scripture, to stand by and for the gospel and to live to the glory of God.'

Evangelicals Now

'It ought to be read by every Christian leader. Highly recommended.'

Evangelical Action

'If I had my way, I would make sure that every potential candidate for the ministry not only read this book through, but also read it through regularly, at least once a year . . . probably one of the most significant of all the Lloyd-Jones works that has ever been published . . . it will give both encouragement and vision to those who are concerned with the cause of the gospel.'

The Churchman

THE PURITANS: THEIR ORIGINS & SUCCESSORS
ISBN 0 85151 496 0
436 pp. Case-bound

'This book is hard to put down; it grips the reader, and to it he will want to return again and again. None can read it without immense profit.'

Evangelical Times

AUTHORITY
ISBN 0 85151 386 7
96 pp. Paperback

'These are addresses given at a conference of students in 1957 and are still of superb value for students and young Christians . . . '

Vox Reformata

'This is a splendid introduction to the whole question of authority and may be studied with profit by the specialist or layman alike.'

The Gospel Magazine

D. MARTYN LLOYD-JONES:
LETTERS 1919–1981
Selected with Notes by Iain H. Murray
ISBN 0 85151 674 2
270 pp. Cloth-bound

'Take this book reverently, and read to be enriched by the depth of spiritual insight and understanding which God graciously gave to his servant . . . Here is a book well-produced, lovely to handle, full of meaty subjects, with a good photograph of M.L.-J. on the dust-cover . . . it is well worth consideration as a "gift to a friend", but put one on your own shelf first!'

Reformed Theological Journal

GOD'S WAY NOT OURS:
Sermons on Isaiah 1:1–18

ISBN 0 85151 753 6
168 pp. Paperback

'A wonderful example of how to expound the Scriptures without fear or compromise but with a heart of longing for man's salvation.'

Evangelical Times

'Both faithful to the text and powerfully applicable to the present situation . . . [These sermons] were preached in 1963, but reading them you would think they had been delivered last Sunday . . . They show how the prophet's word to Israel can be legitimately applied to the whole human race.'

Foundations

D. MARTYN LLOYD-JONES:
THE FIRST FORTY YEARS
Iain H. Murray

ISBN 0 85151 353 0
412 pp. Cloth-bound, illustrated

In the first volume of the authorized biography of Dr Lloyd-Jones, his story is traced from his rural Welsh background to St Bartholomew's Hospital (where, at the age of 23, he was assistant to Sir Thomas Horder, the King's Physician), then, suddenly, at 27, to a struggling Calvinistic Methodist Mission Church in Aberavon, South Wales. He appears successively as schoolboy, dairyman's assistant, political enthusiast, debater, doctor and finally Christian preacher.

Volume 1 takes us to the start of his ministry at Westminster Chapel, London, on the eve of World War II.

'If Dr Lloyd-Jones' life were a novel it would be panned by critics as too unrealistic. Because his life is a historical reality we are left to wonder at the providential energy that could have effected such an astonishing career.'

Christianity Today

D. MARTYN LLOYD-JONES: THE FIGHT OF FAITH

Iain H. Murray

ISBN 0 85151 564 9
862 pp. Cloth-bound, illustrated

Volume 2 of the authorized biography takes us through the years of Dr Lloyd-Jones' ministry in London. During this time he also ministered in British universities and in Europe, the United States and South Africa. Ultimately, through his books, he came to exercise a world-wide ministry.

This volume is more than the biography of one individual. In many ways it is the story of evangelicalism in the twentieth century.

'Rarely is the publication of the biography of a twentieth century minister a significant event. But rarely is the biographee a minister who influenced an entire era the way David Martyn Lloyd-Jones did his . . . Murray is an exceptional biographer. Consistent in style, thorough in content, and stimulating in interaction with his subject, he at times gives a needed corrective of popular misconceptions . . . This biography should be added to the God-called pastor's reading if he wants to understand the times and receive benefit from the life of . . . the twentieth century's most enduring and doctrinally strong pastoral preacher.'

Trinity Journal

'An essential document in twentieth-century church history, for which we may be profoundly grateful.'

Floodtide

'In the limpid prose we have come to expect from Murray, Lloyd-Jones' life and ministry are chronicled with a wealth of personal information . . . We are greatly in Iain Murray's debt for this spiritual feast.'

Ontario Central Baptist Seminary Journal

'I am delighted that Iain Murray has celebrated his life and work in such a worthy manner. Volume 1 was good; volume 2 is better!'

J. I. Packer in *Evangelicals Now*